Amsterdam.

is an artistic heritage centuries
liberal laws and relaxed enviro
tourists in recent decades, the c
than canals and coffee shops.

The legacy of the Dutch Masters lives on, transformed, in a new generation of innovative artists and
designers. The docks and wharfs of the Noord are
examples of abandoned corners that have been
reclaimed and reinvigorated. Even the architecture
has been reinterpreted, with a modern spin on
the classic canal house.

Visitors today can travel to pop-up restaurants on
abandoned islands or dine in 300-year-old green-
houses. Despite its rich history, Amsterdam is
constantly evolving.

But it's the people who shape the city's atmosphere.
In Amsterdam we spoke to gifted personalities:
the local denim king, an urban artist, a celebrated
chef... Our recommendations are complemented by
photographic showcases and in-depth stories from
global and local talents. It's all about original minds
and the creative vibe. Get lost in the sights, smells
and flavours of the city. Get lost in Amsterdam.

Inside the EYE: Known to locals as "the Oyster", the iconic modern architecture of Delugan Meissl symbolises the expansion of the city into a new hot spot: de Noord, the northern part of town. Facing onto the IJ, the stunning EYE Film Institute is something to behold. The adventure begins as soon as you set out — a shuttle boat service takes you there straight from the city centre. Lose yourself in the

various contemporary exhibitions, cuddle up in the comfy yellow two-seater pods to gain access to unlimited archives of films, or discuss art over a drink in the atmospheric café and bar. The Noord does not end there though—make sure to read our neighbourhood section "Docker's Delight" (page 18).
• Eye, Noord, eyefilm.nl

| On the Canal

Every city has a few unexpected hangouts. *Hannekes Boom* is a beachstyle pavilion in the heart of the centre. It's built on an island next to Central Station and you can travel there by boat. During the warmer months the locals come to enjoy a drink in the sand. During the winter, it's the perfect spot to curl up in a comfortable chair next to the fireplace. The lunch and dinner menu changes regularly and has dishes ranging from Dutch mussels to quinoa salad. Stop in any time of year to check out the excellent live music programme.
• Hannekes Boom, Oost, hannekesboom.nl

From Urban Beaches to Secret Bars

Binnen Amsterdam

Night | Cocktails in the Closet

From the outside, *The Butcher* looks like an ordinary hamburger joint. Once you pass the tables and turn right at the fridges, you end up in front of a huge metal door with a peephole. You'll need the password to pass through that door. Good thing you can pave your way by making a reservation for "The Secret Kitchen Of The Butcher". Behind that door is a whole hidden world: an exclusive cocktail bar where well-seasoned bartenders mix the best drinks just for you. Locals and expats come together in this supercool spot.
• The Butcher Bar, De Pijp, the-butcher.com

| Almost Chelsea Market

The opening of *De Hallen* was the talk of town. This former tramshed has been transformed into a creative hub. The vibrant place houses restaurants, stores, an art house movie theatre, a hotel, and *Foodhallen*, the first permanent indoor food market in Amsterdam. The market comprises over 21 stalls from local food producers. It's a serious challenge not to overeat—every stall is as delicious as the next. If the bustle of the market isn't your scene, but you're looking for a bite, check out *Meat West*, an upscale meat-focused restaurant, or the brasserie style restaurant *Halte 3*.
• De Hallen, West, dehallen-amsterdam.nl

Shop | Design Eden

Near the Waterlooplein, famous for its vintage and flower markets you'll find this store for design lovers: Whether it's fashion, home or trinkets, *Hôtel Droog* has it all. They do collaborations with upcoming brands and well-known names from all over the world. This mixture of creative miscellany is housed in a 17th century building of over 700 square metres. On the ground floor you can buy items for your home—the collection carries designer labels from all over the world. Then head to the courtyard—a fairytale-like garden sprouting in the middle of the building. On the upper floor you'll find the restaurant called *Roomservice*. This quirky spot is open for lunch and serves high tea.
• Hôtel Droog, Centrum, hoteldroog.com

Camera Art

Foam is the place to be for anyone interested in photography. This celebrated museum attracts talented camera wielders from all over the globe, housing a vast array of styles. Upcoming artists and world-renowned snappers alike share wall space here, while creatives of all stripes meet to participate in forums and discussions. The building itself is a masterpiece—a mixture of original architecture and modern chrome and glass makes the perfect backdrop for the visual treats on offer. Set next to the canal, the picturesque walk to this gallery, library, bookshop and cafe only adds further to the enchanting visual voyage.
• Foam, Centrum, foam.org

Hunting for Collectibles

There's no better way to get a feel for a city than by taking a stroll through one of its flea markets. If you have a free Saturday don't miss the opportunity to visit the lively *Noordermarkt*. All sorts of second hand treasures are there for you to find. Farmers from all around Amsterdam also set up shop here every week, bringing in the freshest food for you to feast on. Wander into the *Boerenmarkt* part of Noordermarkt and surround yourself with its strong fragrances of meat, herbs and cheese— a surefire way to work up your appetite.
• Noordermarkt, Centrum, noordermarkt-amsterdam.nl

Shop | Love for Sale

Amsterdam is a prime city for passionate shoppers. Beside the Utrechtsestraat and the Nine Streets is the must-visit *Haarlemmerstraat*—and its adjoining Haarlemmerdijk. Check out *Six and Sons, Sukha, Tenue de Nimes, Restored* or *Concrete Matter*—you're sure to find something special.

Six and Sons and *Concrete Matter* focus only on men, both ideal spots for gift shopping. *Sukha* is known for its sustainable products and a very cool interior. To top up energy levels, stop in at *Stach* for a healthy snack or check out *Ibericus*, a specialty store for Spanish cured hams.
• Centrum, several locations, see Index p. 67

Food | Hangover Brunch

After a night on the Amsterdam tiles, the restorative doctor's order is to be found at classic brunch establishment *G's*. The tiny venue in the Jordaan occupies a location that was once a strip club. Aside from the spectacular food, you'll remember G's best for its Bloody Mary—a perfect choice to get the blood circulating again. Limited seating plus the place's popularity led Mister G (that's George) to invent a new concept: *G's Brunch Boat*. Departing twice a day on Saturday and Sunday from in front of the Anne Frank house, it's the best way to tour the Amsterdam canals while eating and drinking. The two-hour boat ride includes a choice of three brunch dishes. Reserve a seat online—or be spontaneous and show up at least 10 minutes before boarding.
• G's Brunch Boat, Centrum, reallyniceplace.com

Katrin Korfmann & Jens Pfeifer
Katrin Korfmann and Jens Pfeifer
have been married since 2005.
Katrin Korfmann is an artist
working in various disciplines—
installation, photography
and video. Her work has been
exhibited internationally in
galleries, museums, alternative art
institutions and public spaces.
Jens Pfeifer is a visual artist who
creates sculptures, drawings
and site-specific work. He is also a
Professor at Rietveld Academie
Amsterdam. The couple lives with
two kids in De Baarsjes

Katrin Korfmann & Jens Pfeifer

Four Eyes Bright

A fairytale-like bicycle trip to Waterland, colourful markets outside the city centre, and all the right spots for the chocolate-addicted—Katrin and Jens know Amsterdam inside out. As creatives and connoisseurs they gravitate towards unique and imaginative spots—they share with us their favourite places to get inspired and tell us where to nab the tastiest food in town

From high culture at Stedelijk Museum (above) to the hight art of apple cake at Winkel 43 (below)

Katrin and Jens, you both moved to Amsterdam over a decade ago. Why? What makes Amsterdam so special?

Katrin: The city is small but totally global. You can reach everything by bike. There are bike paths everywhere…

Jens: Yes, we really connect to the open and global mentality of Amsterdam.

Where do you feel the Amsterdam vibe most in the streets?

Jens: First of all, you should leave the centre behind. Here you meet mostly tourists. I like to cook and to go to the markets. The *Dappermarkt* in the East is typical for Amsterdam: people from the Caribbean, Suriname, Africa or Asia—offering raw or cooked food. A mix like this makes Amsterdam special. But also at *Albert Cuypmarkt*, which tends to be a little more touristic, you can still feel this potpourri of cultures.

Katrin: They sell the best fish in town there.

Jens: True.

Katrin: It's also about the atmosphere. We moved around a lot. Now we are living De Baarsjes, in the West. Lots of Moroccan and Turkish families live here; the neighborhood is so rich in contrast.

Jens: In the neighbourhoods like de Baarsjes, Noord, de Bijlmer, Oost, Bos en Lommer, you can see all the different cultures which make Amsterdam a unique city.

Amsterdam's art scene is rich and robust, but with so much choice it's difficult to know where to start. As artists yourselves, which spots would you suggest to someone visiting the city?

Jens: Of course the classics like *Rijksmuseum* and *Stedelijk* are always worth a visit. What I can recommend: attend a concert at *Concertgebouw*. The old concert hall is beautiful and nowadays they offer a contemporary programme as well.

Katrin: Yes, and the acoustics of the building belong to the world's best.

Jens: Also worth going to is the Museum *Ons' Lieve Heer op Solder*. Behind a characteristic facade lies an original 17th-century hidden church, including the private home.

Katrin: And it's in the middle of today's Red Light District—that's kind of funny. I would also suggest *Kunstverein*—organised by a small group of people but with very interesting projects. *De Appel Arts Centre* and art space *W139* are also worth checking out. And *NASA*, which stands for New Art Space Amsterdam—they have a cinema and a good restaurant in-house.

You have been married for nine years. What are the best places here for a romantic day or evening?

Katrin: There are many small romantic cafés, but we suggest something near the water, or even on the water, like *Pllek*, situated close to NDSM-werf. Delicious food—and you have to go there by boat from Centraal Station so that is already the perfect introduction.

Jens: Or take your love to *Pont 13*, a former ferry boat in the old harbor with delicious food and a great view. Unfortunately it's closed in winter. Or take a walk in the evening through the canals in the area of De 9 Straatjes—sounds cliché but it's a really romantic experience.

Katrin: And if you really want the evening to be a very special one you can also rent a Salonboot for a private candlelit dinner on the canals, or visit *Bar 23* for a cocktail and great view. It is located on the top floor of the Okura Hotel, the best sushi place in town, by the way.

Katrin, from your perspective, if your best friends were visiting, what would the perfect day in Amsterdam look like for you?

We would start with Saturday organic farmers market at Noordermarkt. In this area, the Dutch apple pie at the famous *Winkel 43* is a must. We would then bike to Houthaven and take the ferry to NDSM terrain. Get off and visit the galleries *New Dakota* and *Vous Etes Ici.* Have a coffee at Pllek and visit the NDSM-loods, a huge hangar turned into artists' studios. We would then cycle to the *EYE* Film Institute to watch a movie. Then we'd take the ferry from there to Centraal Station and stop to people-watch at the Zeedijk, Amsterdam's Chinatown.

In the evening, we'd eat at one of the several restaurants around Westerstraat, like *Toscanini*, to finally end up playing pool and drinking at *Club8* around the corner from where we live.

Jens, same question: what would you do if your best friend from abroad were visiting?

I always enjoy the opportunity to explore the city when a friend comes for a visit—something I rarely do on my own anymore. I see the city moving and growing and I'm interested in the new developments in urban planning and architecture. So we would take bikes, of course—the best way to travel in the city—and go through Westerpark where we'd stop at one of the cafés for a late breakfast. Then we'd move on through the Houthaven and take a ferry to take us to Noord, which is divided from the rest of the city by the IJ canal. We'd see the NDSM-werf, the EYE Museum, maybe a pop-up gallery, and go for lunch in one of the many new cafés and restaurants in the Noord. Then back with the ferry again towards the city centre to cycle through the narrow streets near the canals. I'm a chocolate addict, so we'd definitely get some "bonbons" at *Chocolaterie Pompadour, Puccini Bomboni* or *Unlimited Delicious,* to name just a few. After that we'd hang out in Vondelpark or go to one of the museums. Five o'clock is "Borrel-time". Every pub ("Kroeg") has a variety of finger food to accompany your beer or wine. The most popular are Bitterballen, Kroket, Frikandel, Ossenworst, or plain cheese with mustard. But a herring from one of the many small stands on the streets is also a typically Dutch and very delicious alternative if you don't want to hang out in a bar too early. Amsterdam offers almost every cuisine of the world— the choice is difficult! I like the Thai restaurant on the Overtoom a lot: *Sawaddee Ka.* Sometimes though, we'd just end up in *De Engelse Reet* to catch up on each other's news. It's my absolute favourite bar—very old, very small, with many different beers and liquors and the most friendly and knowledgeable staff ever. And they don't play music!

And what is your current favourite place for dining out together?

Katrin: During the week we really like *Café Cook*. It's a nice restaurant in our neighborhood with great food and a vivid square out front.

Jens: For special occasions we love to go to *Restaurant Merkelbach*. It offers an innovative kitchen and a stunning atmosphere.

Katrin: Yes, that restaurant is located in Huize Frankendael, which is a super-nice country estate with a park and regular exhibitions held by the foundation.

Restaurant Merkelbach is the perfect Sunday place: exhibitions, a location in beautiful Park Frankendael, slow food and credit cards only

Westen, a super playground.

Jens: On the beach, places like Wijk an Zee or Bloemendaal. But we come here in fall when the big party is over and it's getting more quiet.

Is there another place nearby that's worth travelling out of the city to see?

Jens: Definitely Waterland—the great nature experience! Quiet, authentic and with beautiful villages.

Katrin: You can go there by bike. It's a nice trip. Rent a bike or car and go to Broek en Waterland; it's a village from a fairytale.

Jens: And go further to Uitdam, a small village directly on the Markenmeer. Here you can go swimming in the summer, or bike on the bank and head to *Thetuin t'Einde* in Zuiderwoude for coffee and cake.

Katrin: And then head on to Holysloot and have dinner at the former school building: *Het Schoolhuis*. From there you can bike to the ferry in Amsterdam Noord and take the boat to the centre.

Thank you for all these insights. Seems like Amsterdam is a perfect city. Or is something missing?

Katrin: Just one thing: A "Kunsthal" would be perfect.

Jens: Yes, we need more places for contemporary art.

Where do you go if you want to get inspired?

Katrin & Jens: We both like cycling to the studio.

Jens: Perfect for sorting out your ideas.

Katrin: Great to just clear your mind.

Where do you relax?

Katrin: Have a walk around Westerpark. Go to *Buurtboederij* for a drink or one of the different activities they offer. The park is also perfect for kids. We have two. And everybody who comes with their little ones should go to Het Woeste

Noord

Docker's Delight

| Shop | Vintage Meets Industrial

Woodies at Berlin & Woodies Classic Boat Services is more than just a vintage design shop. The creative couple behind the concept is inspired by film, fashion, architecture and culture. Esther has an eye for detail, mixing and matching old and new, and designing furniture to specification. Partner Huib brings Esther's designs to life, building what she draws and creating fittings for the boats. In the showroom are Polish light fixtures, antique rugs, 1950s settees, design bookcases and upcycled cupboards. Outside on the quay, a couple of schooners wait for refurbishment. The huge warehouses of *Neef Louis and Van Dijk and Ko* stand side by side. Each is an Aladdin's cave of industrial, design and vintage furniture filled with rows and rows of

household articles from yesteryear—relics from another age. It's the perfect place to find that special something to give your home a unique, rustic feel. If you're on low budget, find a bargain at *De Lokatie*. The shop sells top-notch second-hand household goods and furniture. The *Blom en Blom* brothers are passionate about forgotten items from forgotten places. They collect, restore and redesign furniture and light fittings from derelict factories in former East Germany. Industrial items from abandoned eras are given a new lease on life in modern homes. The story behind each artefact is told in an accompanying "passport" so its rich history lives on.

• Noord, several locations, see Index p. 67

Summer Nights

Picture yourself dining outdoors surrounded by nature, water, space and light—on an island. The Lighthouse Island (Vuurtoreneiland) is a listed UNESCO World Heritage Site. The abandoned defences are home to a herd of sheep and a high-class summer restaurant in a glass house. A five-hour round trip by boat is included in the price of the meal: guests arrive from Amsterdam on a historic ferry, over the river, through the locks and past the old fishing village of Durger-dam, along the dike. The restaurant is open from May to September. Book in advance to guarantee seats and a spectacular experience.
• Zomerrestaurant Vuurtoreneiland, vuurtoreneiland.nl

Culture · Night · Food **Unknown Arts**

At the end of the 19th century, Amsterdam's gentry used to cross the IJ to listen to concerts in the *Tolhuistuin* (Toll House Gardens). For a cen-tury, the grounds have been hidden behind high fences. Now the gardens have been unlocked and the park is once again a venue for concerts. Inside, the 1970s pavilion has been turned into a multicultural centre. It houses the *THT Restaurant* (photo), the Paradiso Noord club, a gallery, and dance studios. Once hidden from the world itself, the Tolhuistuin makes what was previously inaccessi-ble available to all.
• Tolhuistuin, Buiksloterweg 5c, Noord, tolhuistuin.nl

Food **Fish Tales**

Once upon a time, Amsterdam was a bustling fishing port on the Zuiderzee. Today, the city is cut off from the sea by dams and dikes—but fish is still a popular specialty. *Restaurant Stork* has a prime location with a riverside terrace on "De Overkant" (the other side). The original structure of the former machine factory has been left intact, giving the interior an industrial-chic ambiance. A three-course meal with wine will cost you around 50 euros. Stork uses sustainably caught, seasonal fish—so you can indulge in a seafood platter without feeling guilty.
• Restaurant Stork, Gedempt Hamerkanaal 201, Noord, restaurantstork.nl

Culture · Food · Nights | **Northern Lights**

In the 1950s, the NDSM was Europe's biggest ship-yard. After its closure in 1984, squatters took over the abandoned docks, followed by artists, creatives and entrepreneurs. First *Café Noorderlicht* opened, drawing an alternative crowd, and the Wharf became an established venue for festivals. Now an art city and indoor market occupy the spacious halls. The derelict dockland has become a popular creative hub with media companies and hotels: the budget Botel, classy Brooklyn and Faralda Crane Hotel have all set up shop in the area. But in spite of its gentrification, the *NDSM Wharf* is still a rough diamond where industrial heritage stands side by side with chic restaurants like *Bistro Noord* and trendy bars like *Pllek*.

• NDSM Wharf, Noord, ndsm.nl

Culture · Food · Nights | **Modern Hippies**

Café De Ceuvel has fast become one of Amsterdam's coolest hot spots. Stashed away on a secluded canal with a sunny waterside terrace, this infectiously happy place attracts a crowd of twenty-somethings and houses a robust cultural programme. Guests can enjoy various presentations, workshops, yoga, films, live bands and local DJs. Originally the site of a disused boatyard, it was so polluted that commercial parties were not interested in developing it. A multidisciplinary team of idealists won a competition to exploit the property, and went to work turning it into an eco-friendly village of workspaces. It now consists of 17 boats on dry land, connected by an elevated boardwalk, and the grounds have been planted with willows and grasses which will cleanse the soil over the course of the ten-year project. It was nominated for the Dutch Design Award in 2014 immediately after opening. The food is organic and transparently sourced—with as much as possible home-grown on the roof orchard in self-made planters. The aim is 100% sustainability. De Ceuvel is also home to the Dutch Weed Burger, made from seaweed—a healthy, tasty, and fast superfood. Everything you see at De Ceuvel is recycled, crowdfunded and built using the help of volunteers—so, it's not surprising the modern-day, marooned Noah's Arks are making waves in eco-circles.

• Café de Ceuvel, Korte Papaverweg 4, Noord, cafedeceuvel.nl

Food | Taste Factory

The restaurateurs of *Hotel de Goudfazant* and *Café Modern* are pioneers in creating off-the-beaten-track, good-quality restaurants. But nothing is what it seems… Hotel de Goudfazant is not a hotel. And Café Modern only opens for dinner. The combination of haute cuisine, good service and unlikely location is a hit. Hotel de Goudfazant is in a quayside garage in an industrial area. A Ferrari and a Porsche are parked in the back. A space for private parties is partitioned off from the restaurant by a long concrete-surfaced bar with a magnificent glass-bottle chandelier hanging from the ceiling. Otherwise, the spacious structure has been left unchanged. The open kitchen serves a seasonal menu of delicious good-value dishes like wild boar terrine, spring chicken, and cantarelle spinach risotto. The tables and chairs would look more at home in a 1950s canteen than an upmarket restaurant, and the roll-down shutters are opened up on hot summer days onto a broad riverside quay. *Café Modern* is located in a former bank; downstairs you can still see the vaults. The restaurant serves a set five-course menu which changes weekly. It's in the historic Van de Pek neighbourhood, just walking-distance from the ferry. In the daytime, the same premises are used by *Jacques Jour*, which serves breakfast and lunch. Upstairs is a tiny boutique hotel, Sweet Dreamz. The surrounding area is also undergoing a facelift—when it's finished a local market will be just around the corner.

• Hotel de Goudfazant, Aambeeldstraat 10 H, hoteldegoudfazant.nl; Café Modern, Meidoornweg 2, Noord, modernamsterdam.nl

Jason Denham

Denim's Capital

Jason Denham
This Englishman is the creative mind behind internationally successful jeans brand "Denham". After working several years for English designer Joe Casley-Hayford, Denham set up his own consultancy in Amsterdam called Clinic before founding the jeans brand Blue Blood. In 2008 after extensive travel around Europe, US and Japan, he started "Denham", opening up shop in Amsterdam

Shops for vintage clothing, temples for sneaker freaks or gift stores for men—designer Jason Denham knows all the places showing a passion for authentic products and fine details. Most of his favourite spots in Amsterdam are around his design studios in Prinsengracht. Take a stroll with Mr. "Denim" Denham

Concrete Matters will provide you with anything, ranging from vintage paper planes to stylish crowbars

How is the real Amsterdammer dressed best? And does the style express the atmosphere of the city?

Every Amsterdammer is dressed in jeans. It is the city of bikes, and jeans are the perfect match. Now that Autumn weather is coming everyone is starting to layer up in leather jackets and tailored Crombie coats.

What are the best shops for local designers?

Obviously *Denham*, we are local designers! Visit our men's store at Prinsengracht, our women's store at Runstraat and of course our flagship store on Hobbemastraat.

Haha… of course. But apart from Denham—where would you suggest to your friends to go to buy quality casual clothing in Amsterdam?

Amsterdam is full of great boutiques and vintage stores. I suggest you check out *Tenue De Nimes*, *Six & Sons*, *Tommy Page Vintage* and *Concrete Matters* for boys toys; also *Baskèts* for the sneaker freaks.

Are there any areas you would suggest to go for a stroll around the city?

Nine Streets (De Negen Straatjes) is the best place in the city for the overall experience—bars, cafes, shopping…

Jason Denham enjoys Nacional for dinner but the new hotspot is also open for breakfast and lunch

What are your favourite food places in town—for lunch and for dinner?

For lunch I recommend *Foodware*. And for dinner *Nacional*.

You are English, so it won't sound weird if I ask you where would you'd go for a good drink in Amsterdam?

Amsterdam is the perfect drinking city. It's a city like in a village so everywhere is easy and accessible, everywhere is open late, and pretty much everywhere is friendly. The latest new hotspot is Nacional, but all the small brown cafes and brown bars are great.

Where do you go if you if want to relax in or out of town?

Amsterdam has great parks in the city: Vondelpark, Westerpark and Amsterdamse Bos are great places to switch off, relax and get lost.

What is the next city we should get lost in, and why?

Definitely Tokyo, the most exciting city in the world!

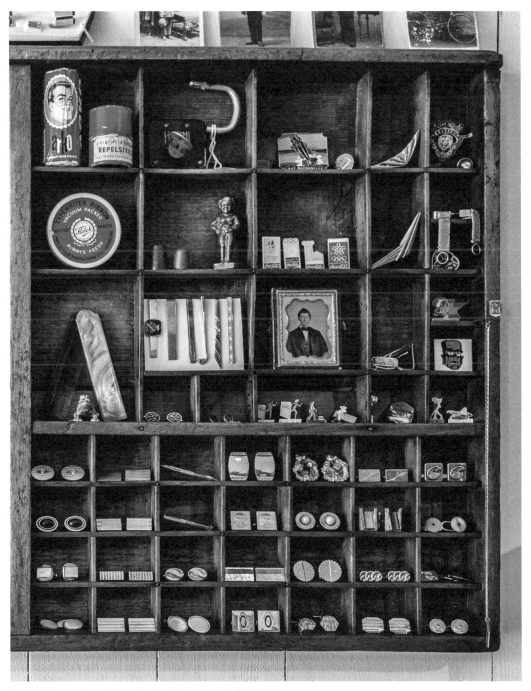

Tommy Page stocks a unique selection of last century's fashion items

Cycling
City on Wheels

In Amsterdam, the first thing you notice is the prevalence of bicycles.
In fact, the city has more of the contraptions than it does people.
The vehicle accounts for more than half of all trips within the centre—
more than walking, driving and public transport trips combined.
It seems as though no Amsterdammer's life is complete without their
two-wheeled friend. The city and the bicycle share a rich common
history, intertwined with politics, tradition and innovation...

At the end of the 19th century, bikes were expensive and therefore only used by the privileged upper class in Amsterdam. Both men and women took lessons on how to cycle with elegance and sophistication: women would learn how to mount their bikes in a lady-like fashion, and men would be instructed to tip their hats to salute other cyclists. In the 1920s, the rise of local factories made bicycles very affordable. The Calvinist approach of the Dutch made the bike an easy choice: it was a cheap and practical way to get around and to transport goods from place to place. After the Great Depression and World War II, the bike's popularity grew further and became the main mode of transport for the majority of Amsterdammers.

Politics also played a large role in the city becoming so bicycle-friendly. Politicians realised that cycling was the future of their growing city and began to take action. Campaigns for safer streets, bike paths and restrictions on motorised vehicles meant that, bit by bit, the transportation system was transformed. Locals have fought for their beloved bicycles as well: in the 1960s, when the car became affordable and was seen as "the vision of the future" (and the bike as something of the past), a pro-bicycle movement was born. The Provo movement started the first free bike sharing programme in the world—50 bikes were painted white and left on the street for people to use. However, the concept didn't succeed, as it was against the law to leave a bike unlocked on the street. Even though all the white bikes were impounded by the police, the Provos managed to put the bicycle back on the political agenda. Another battle for bike rights was won with the "Law on Road Traffic". It states that the "strong participant in traffic" (a motorised vehicle) automatically assumes liability in an accident with a "weak participant in traffic" (i.e. a pedestrian, cyclist, non-motorised vehicle). In other words: the bike rules the roads.

Amsterdammers are very proud of their traditional Dutch bike, which has been the most common in use since the beginning of the 20th century. The Dutch call them, "grandma" or "grandpa" bikes. They are single-speed and sport a back-brake. These bikes are usually black, made of steel and rusty—and most have a squeaky wheel and an almost-flat back tire. You sit upright, so you can easily see the traffic or chat with a friend cycling next to you. Every bike has a chain guard and fenders on the wheels, making it possible to wear everyday clothes (or a suit and tie, dress or high heels), even in the rain. Amsterdammers often accessorize their bike with silk flowers, an oversized, loud bike bell, or an extra-large wooden crate for hauling groceries.

Because of its strong frame, the Dutch bike can carry more than one person. You often see people sitting on the rear racks, or "dinking". Parents can cart multiple children around, with a front seat attached to the handlebars and a back seat attached to the rear rack. Cargo bicycles ("bakfiets") are also popular among young families. With these you can easily take your three kids, dog, and picnic basket to the Vondelpark. Around Amsterdam you'll also notice the hoards of men cycling on female bikes ("omafiets"). This trend of men riding women's bikes is thought to have started during World War II, when the Nazis occupied the Netherlands. Men were forced to hand over their bikes—in total, 55,000 were commandeered. However, the Germans were not interested in female bikes, so instead of facing the threat of losing their bike, many Dutch men rode female bikes and left theirs at home. Today teenage boys ride their omafietsen to school or along the canals to impress girls.

Another way the Dutch express themselves through their choice of bicycle is to pick a model from a local business. Roetz is a popular Amsterdam brand that produces recycled, trendy bikes. They upcycle old bikes, picking the best frames and making them as good as new. They are always red or grey, with white, cork-gripped handlebars and leather saddles. For something a bit out-of-the-ordinary, wooden bikes from Bough Bike and bamboo models from Black Star Bikes are also popular choices. Similar to the Roetz bike, they're made using sustainable materials and stand out because of their signature styles.

Amsterdam is still a trend-setting city in the cycling world. It's seen as a bike utopia, as many cities around the globe are trying to follow suit and become more bicycle friendly themselves. Eventually the hope is that Amsterdam will no longer be "the bicycle capital of the world", and rather just one of many, but it will always be remembered as a pioneer. Until then, Amsterdammers will proudly pedal along on their squeaky-wheeled steel horses, patiently waiting for the rest of the world to catch up.

Text and pictures by Meredith Glaser, Joni Uhlenbeck and Aude de Prelle of Amsterdam Cycle Chic

An Amsterdammer feeling at home on the back of a bike

Amie Dicke

Obvious Secrets

Amie Dicke

Most people expect artists to paint, but that's the one thing this Dutch visual artist doesn't do. Her artistic expression is more diverse, expressed with sculpture, works on paper and research into found objects that share a common essence. Through her works, Dicke subtly brings light to the unseen and forgotten—it's about shifting perspectives. She challenges our perceptions of both the everyday and the extraordinary. After graduating from Willem de Kooning Academy in her hometown of Rotterdam, Dicke moved to New York City for a few years before returning to the Netherlands to Amsterdam eight years ago. Today, she is deeply rooted to the city she calls home

Amie's work shows that even amid consensus, our perceptions are ultimately our own. Looking at Amsterdam through her eyes, ordinary tourist attractions become secret hide-outs and insider spots become accessible. Her favorite places are as unique as her studio, which is located in a church (it still holds occasional services). The altar serves as a conference table. Amsterdam is not only Amie Dicke's home and workplace, it's her source of inspiration, too

You are originally from Rotterdam. What made you move to Amsterdam?

Love and work. My boyfriend already worked here so he was commuting back and forth between the cities to make sure that we saw each other. And my home gallery is located here, so moving here felt like a logical consequence.

Amsterdam has many nice neighborhoods. Which one did you decide on?

The so-called Plantage Buurt. We still live in the same place. It's a very nice area: close to the zoo, Rijksacademie and Hortus Botanicus. It's not too crowded with tourists and it has a lot of green spaces.

As an artist you express yourself visually. How would you show the essence of Amsterdam in one image?

Through a photograph of a bicycle bell stuck in asphalt.

To illustrate that cycling plays an important role in Amsterdam's everyday life?

Yes. It's no cliché–there are a lot of people cycling in Amsterdam. It makes up the feel of the city. It's even something that I really miss when I am away, as being on a bike is a very essential part of my life in Amsterdam—it's how you get around. But the streets in Amsterdam are still old and paved with cobblestones, so you'll get shaken when biking here. That's why bicycle bells fall off so often. Especially the tops of the bells. Every Dutch person knows that you'll lose your bell once in a while. It's normal. If you're aware of them, you can see them lying around everywhere. I've been obsessed with them for a year and always picked them up when I find them. Even when I've been in a hurry, quickly going from A to B, I've stopped when I've seen one, manoeuvred between the traffic, gotten it and put it into my collection. I have more than 100. The ones I like most are the ones that get stuck in the pavement because a car drove over it. But I can't take these ones with me as I can't prise them out. For me, they are the piercings of the city. They are wonderful, strange signs that tell of damage, loss or an accident. So this is one of the things that I tell people who come to Amsterdam: "Try to look out for the bike bells in the streets. This is the typical Amsterdam. But it happens in the periphery of your vision. Don't try to search for them, you will see them along the way. It's impossible to find them deliberately."

Where would you bike to with a guest in Amsterdam for a short visit?

To the *Oude Kerk*. It's the oldest church of Amsterdam and currently the oldest building in the city. It dates back to the 14th century. It's in the middle of the Red Light District, surrounded by sex, drugs and a lot of tourists. In fact, it's almost impossible to bike there as it's so crowded. But it's worthwhile to cut one's way through. Most people go there to visit the grave of Saskia van Uylenburgh, Rembrandt's wife. But I go there for another reason. Just when you enter the church, there are two spiral staircases. One is on the right side, another is on the left side. One is open, the other one is closed. If you go to the closed one, you can press your spine against the spine of the staircase. You don't need to walk up to do that. You have to do it when you are still on the ground floor. When you stand there and look up, you get the most wonderful vertigo.

Your studio is at the Church De Duif at the Prinsengracht. You seem to have some kind of connection to churches...

Maybe, yes. At the same time it's also a coincidence. The Oude Kerk is still working as a church, although it's also rented out sometimes as it tries to find its position in today's society. And that's what I find so interesting. People still love the church as a place to sightsee and reflect, but they have mainly lost their religion. So how can we deal with these buildings today? Can we find a new soul for them? Their structures still breathe meaning and even consolation to us.

What about Amsterdam is similarly touching for you?
To walk around the *Hortus Botanicus* in summer nights. Of course, the botanical gardens are also nice from the inside during daytime, but there is something magical that you can only experience at a late hour: you'll hear wonderful sounds that may remind you of birds—it's something like whistling. But it's frogs, in fact. I've never heard anything as magnificent as that. And in the winter I love to bike through the Vondelpark at nightfall. Then, the lights in the park are not on yet. So, you only see the bike lights. And they are moving around in the air to the movement of the bikes. That's very funny. And dogs have lights on them, too.

As an artist, you probably know where to see good exhibitions.
Yes. I recommend *Stigter van Doesburg*. That's the gallery I'm working with. And also *Galerie Fons Welter*, *Annet Gelink Gallery* and *Martin van Zomeren*. They are all located in the Jordaan district and not too far from each other— perfect to walk around all of them.

And what place do you propose for food?
I just discovered the *Hoftuin*. It's a new restaurant in an old building just behind the Hermitage museum. You can have a perfect lunch there.

And where do you like to go to dinner?
My favorite place is the *Merkelbach* restaurant. It's located in an old land house, has a wonderful garden and good food. Especially the smoked fish is great. But you should make a reservation to ensure you get a seat. If you just like to walk in somewhere easily, I suggest the *Brasserie Schiller* at the Rembrandtplein. It's a crowded area, but it's a nice place to have simple food and good wine. You can have everything from a good stamppot to pasta. It's not starred chef food, but I like the laid-back atmosphere.

Talking about traditional food, which is your favorite traditional dish?
It is not a dish, but I like drop, licorice, and—this may sound disgusting now, especially as part of the same sentence—herring. Especially the pickled ones.

Where do you get the best herring?
There are little fish shops all over the place. But the best ones, surely, are on Utrechtsestraat.

Amie Dicke's studio is located at the Church De Duif in Prinsengarcht, equipped with a handy spot for a siesta

Contemporary Dutch Architecture
Skin and Bones

Perhaps no other nation has had as big an influence on contemporary architecture as The Netherlands. With firms like OMA and MVRDV leading the charge, Dutch architecture has become a worldwide industry, with buildings popping up in Europe, North America, and especially China

Though Koolhaas is the biggest name and perhaps the most prolific architect on the Dutch scene, there are several important firms following in his wake, including MVRDV, UNstudio, Wiel Arets, JHK Architecten, West 8, and Neutelings Riedijk. At first glance these firms have little in common, save for geography and a loose affiliation with Modernism, but they actually have deep historical and theoretical links. The strands connecting them together aren't just in books, either; they make their mark on every aspect of the building projects, from organisation to form.

One of the distinguishing characteristics of Dutch architecture is the focus on the façade of buildings. These exterior envelopes are articulated with windows, patterned with luxurious materials, and pulled into taut continuous surfaces, even if they sit on fairly unadventurous boxy structures. This focus shows a view that architecture is a wrapper and backdrop for activity. Programme (what happens inside spaces) and circulation are paramount: once the structure is designed, other interior spaces are often left open, with the boundaries between interior and exterior left as the only sites for adornment. As Koolhaas once said, "As more and more architecture is finally unmasked as the mere organization of flow—shopping centres, airports—it is evident that circulation is what makes or breaks public architecture."

Tracing the origins of this programme-and-facade architecture can be a bit tricky, since it has been percolating through architecture discourse for quite some time. But in the case of Koolhaas, we can follow it back to his 1972 thesis for the AA School in London. For this project, called "Exodus", Koolhaas incorporated concepts and forms previously explored by cybernetic architects like Cedric Price and megastructural systems as seen in Metabolist design to create a dystopian vision for London: a giant wall cutting across the city that serves as a refuge for its beleaguered citizens. The wall divides internal spaces based on activity, and creates a gigantic surface around these programmes. (One only need look at Koolhaas' more recent books Project Japan: Metabolism Talks and Re:CP to see more examples of these influences.)

The idea of treating a surface as the most important component of design goes back even further within the Dutch tradition itself, all the way to De Stijl and Theo van Doesburg's avant-garde designs (as well as those of Oud and van Eesteren) from the 1920s. Van Doesburg created houses with completely open interiors, with no boundaries between spaces, circulation, or rooms. He adorned the exterior surfaces with fields of colour, each panel dynamically placed to seem as if in motion. These exterior panels separate the interior programme from the world beyond; the colour is ostensibly

The private houses in Oostelijk Havengebied (Eastern Docklands) are a prime example of Van Doesburg's heritage

the result of the energy of the interior slamming into the architectural wrapping surface.

Van Doesburg's friend and rival, Piet Mondrian, illustrates this idea more clearly with his paintings. Largely unified in terms of motif (black intersecting lines) and colour, Mondrian's compositions present a universal vision of the world, or rather, "represent the world's underlying pattern, reality, and energy", as Mondrian writes in "Plastic Art and Pure Plastic Art". Each canvas becomes a single portal through what appears to be real, down to the universal field of colour.

So then, the exterior surface of a building becomes an index of the programme on the interior, containing activity within a wrapper, but still being perturbed by the energy within. In the work of OMA, this manifests as separate surfaces, interior and exterior, covered in single materials, often differing within the same building. Take the Rotterdam Kunsthal: here, wood forms the steps and focal wall of the auditorium, a red concrete line faces the street, and channel glass forms the entry facade. Other buildings, such as the CCTV Tower, appear as simple volumes arranged in a simple form; the interior activity is shown through the delicate structural lattice by day, and at night by the office cubes that shine through the dematerialised glass exterior.

One of the major ways architects achieve these articulated Dutch exteriors is through continuous surfaces that weave in and out of a building. In OMA's Educatorium, a single edge slices through the building multiple times, curving from floor to ceiling at one end, like a ribbon. The firm's TVCC building (the one that caught on fire next door to the CCTV Tower) consists of glass-clad floorplates squeezed inside of a metallic casing, the glass seemingly revealed only by the intersecting of the metallic volume of both facades. This same surface-splitting parti appears in UNstudio's Mirai House, where a continuous white surface was cut to reveal the windows of the office spaces.

This programme-and-surface-based approach to architecture has spread beyond the Netherlands into the work of many contemporary firms including BIG (Denmark) and Herzog & de Meuron (Switzerland), both of which adopt continuous surfaces, and well-adorned boxes as a key to an architectural vocabulary. This approach seems to work well in a world where the movement of goods, people, and information accelerates and becomes ever more important. As Koolhaas once tweeted, "People can inhabit anything. And they can be miserable in anything and ecstatic in anything. Architecture has nothing to do with it." But if the rich tradition of Dutch design—and Koolhaas' buildings particularly— is anything to go by, then that's not entirely true. Rather, architecture provides the setting for our lives, the enclosure within which we are free to be anything.

Text by AJ Artemel. AJ Artemel is a designer and a writer on architecture, urbanism and the built environment. He holds a master's degree in architecture, and his work has previously appeared in blogs and publications such as Architizer, The Atlantic Cities, CLOG, and Gizmodo, among others. An older version of this article was published on architizer.com

Through the Eyes of a Flâneur

A photo showcase from Thomas Manneke

Following in the Dutch tradition of social documentary, paved by predecessors like Van Elsken, Thomas Manneke captures real life in Amsterdam. The images depict an alternative side to the capital. By photographing daily life, he presents an uncertain, solitary and almost desolate city. A world where time stands still and where subjects seem to vanish into their environments

Esther Dorhout Mees

Dynamic Design

Esther Dorhout Mees reveals the most fashionable hangouts and her favourite shops in town, sharing the real Amsterdam fashion experience. Explore designer shops as well as the alternative vintage stores that spice up the Dutch capital's unique style. And find something to do whether it's indulging in a designer shopping spree or going out for drinks after a long day of activity

Where do you see Amsterdam in the fashion world?

I think we are a city where we're okay with everything and anything. You can see that just looking around now as well. I think that in that sort of environment it creates an atmosphere where people dare to experiment and search for what makes you "you". So I feel that creates a beautiful mixture of interesting creators—in fashion, but also outside of fashion.

For instance, in interior design you have *Droog*—everything is brought back to the essence of what a product is, or should be, and in the most innovative ways.

What would you consider the up-and-coming fashion areas of Amsterdam?

It's always moving, really, and it's usually areas where things are happening—not only fashion-wise but in all areas, so new interesting cafés or restaurants that mix with concept stores and fashion.

And as Amsterdam isn't that big, I feel that the interesting stores are scattered throughout the city. But areas that are changing into interesting places are, for instance, the North of Amsterdam, if you take the little boats to the other side of the water. Also Amsterdam West is changing with the big tramremise that has been transformed into an industrial meeting spot with restaurants, terraces, a hotel, a fashion library, TV studios, and shops and studios for designers. It's changed the atmosphere around it immediately.

Since you're a designer you must have a good idea of shops in that area: what would you recommend in Amsterdam?

I love different shops for different things. For a nice blend of designers and a more international atmosphere I like *SPRMRKT*. Then for mixture

of interior design and fashion I love *Frozen Fountain*. For my love of Scandinavia, as I lived in Copenhagen for a long time when I was working for Bruuns Bazaar, I love the little stores of *Rika*. Her Rika Home is also lovely. Even though she is really big around the world, she's kept a beautiful, typically Scandinavian store where you feel at home. It can sometimes remind me of Helena Christensen's store in New York, Butik. For jewellery I love *Leonore* in the Utrechtsestraat. She has a beautiful mixture of delicate jewelry, also Scandinavian. One of my favourites from Copenhagen, only sold in Leonore: Jane Konig.

Where do you usually go shopping?

I go to the places I just mentioned, but also love to just walk around in the Nine Little Streets where there are lots of little cute stores, that I never really remember but can always find lovely things there. There are also a lot of second-hand places. My favourite is *Laura Dols*; go there to find yourself in a couple of different areas at the same time. It's mixed with cafés and coffee bars—nice for a break, if you need one! Even though it's getting more commercial over the last couple of years the atmosphere is still good.

Where in the city would I find the most fashionable people? Any specific hangouts?

Roest in East—it's a perfect hangout place next to the water. *Mossel & Gin* at Westergas Terrain for your best seafood dishes. The *Conservatorium Hotel* for more upscale drinks and dinners in a beautiful environment. *Quartier Puttain* in the Red Light District; they have the best coffee and when you order one you'll get a chip for the jukebox so you can pick out

From cocktail dresses to shoes: Laura Dols specialises in 1950s clothing

Where do you go to get inspired?
I like to be alone for that... walking around the city really early in the morning or really late at night, that would be in summer of course (laughs). But there is something magical about a busy city that comes to a stop at those moments, and you feel it is just your own for a little while. I also love drawing. I make complete books, paintings and illustrations before and during the development of a collection. Sometimes the collection inspires me or it can be the other way around as well. So it is always changing and moving up until the very last moments!

Ideally, where would you go for dinner, drinks and after-drinks to celebrate a successful show?
That would be at the *Westerpark*, but that also has to do with the fact that my shows are in the Gashouder at the Westerpark, and as those days are so hectic we all—my whole team—want to go somewhere nearby and still stay in the atmosphere of that day. There are a lot of different, really nice places at the Westergasterrein, and we mix them up every time. Either *Westerliefde*, which is pretty much in the middle of the fashion week madness, but if we want to be somewhere a bit more quiet and relaxed we go to *Pacific* or *Café Amsterdam*. For cocktails I like *Tales And Spirits* and *Door 74*—they are both more in the centre of Amsterdam.

your own song. Also, close to that, you have the *Schenkerij*. It has this lovely rose garden built against the Oude Kerk. It's this little hidden gem that I love to go to lately.

Where would you recommend to a designer in Amsterdam looking to buy fabric?
I hardly ever buy my materials in Holland actually. But there is this small, but famous, store that everybody knows in Amsterdam called: *A. Boeken*. They have a mixture of everything and anything you might need. So if you're in need of good scissors or zippers and don't have any time, this is the place to go.

Above: The Roest combines laid-back beach atmosphere with culture and clubbing
Below: Art meets fashion at SPRMRKT with collections by Boris Bidjan Saberi, Rick Owens or Damir Doma

East of Eden

Shop | **Capital Concepts**

Amsterdam locals adore concept stores. Even in residential neighbourhoods you'll find these retail havens with unique clothing, accessory, and home living collections. Once your run-of-the-mill working-class neighbourhood, De Pijp has transformed itself into a lively and eclectic shopping hub. *Anna + Nina* is a cabinet of lady-like curiosities collected by two women with impeccable taste. The store offers a selection of jewellery, homewares, gifts and accessories. Just around the corner, you'll find *Cottoncake*. Decked out all in white, this elegant split-level store (pictured) is easy on the eyes. On the top floor you can enjoy a cup of coffee, breakfast or lunch—all organic. Downstairs, browse through the edgy, changing collection—Scandinavian clothing brands sit beside one-off art pieces and quirky accessories. *Hutspot* is the largest concept store in Amsterdam. Here you'll find a vast array of carefully selected brands. The owners experiment regularly, using bits of the store to host everything from pop-up barber shops to cooking classes for kids. Head to the top floor to refuel with some lunch and coffee.
• De Pijp, several locations, see Index p. 67

All neighbourhoods in Amsterdam have their own local coffee bars. The best in De Pijp is the *Scandinavian Embassy* located across from the Sarphatipark. The beans are roasted in Amsterdam and are sourced mostly from Africa or South America. At the Embassy coffee meets food and fashion in a Scandinavian inspired interior. With wooden details and wild flowers on the tables it's a cosy place to enjoy your drink with a cake, lunch or the warm daily special.
• Scandinavian Embassy, Sarphatipark 34, De Pijp, scandinavianembassy.nl

Food | Vitamin Reload

Sla, meaning "salad", is exactly what you'll find on the menu at this delightfully nutritious spot. All ingredients used at Sla are organic and sourced locally when possible. The salad menu is seasonal and offers the healthiest produce. You can also create your own salad by choosing exactly what you like from the salad bar. Make sure to try the red, green and orange juices! Sla's tasteful interior is a mix of wood, brick walls, plants galore and a greenhouse frame as the salad bar. On sunny days the terrace is the best place to be.
• Sla, Ceintuurbaan 149, De Pijp, ilovesla.com.

Food | Haven for Sinners

There are restaurants you go to for the slick interior or because they're the "places to be". Then there are those—like *Restaurant Sinne*—that win you over with something more simple, but harder to achieve: top-notch food, the best wines and excellent service. At the Ceintuurbaan, this is a place that from the outside might not claim your attention. But once inside you'll experience the professionalism and passion that has recently earned Sinne a Michelin star. Despite the accolade, the restaurant has not raised its prices: Sinne offers three to six-course menus starting at 35 euros per person. Book ahead to ensure you try this upscale but reasonably priced treasure, cited by some as the very best Amsterdam has to offer.
• Sinne, Ceintuurbaan 342, De Pijp, restaurantsinne.nl

Day and Night

From morning to evening *Bar Bukowski* is a favourite café for locals. The warm weather months demand appreciation of its sunny terrace. Squeeze in at one of the picnic tables and enjoy some drinks and finger food. Later in the afternoon Bar Bukowski fills up with friends catching up after their workdays are over. The café is connected to *Henry's Bar*, a pop-up cocktail bar open Fridays and Saturdays—stop by to sample their delicious specialty cocktails.
• Bar Bukowski & Henry's Bar, Oosterpark 10–11, Oost, barbukowski.nl

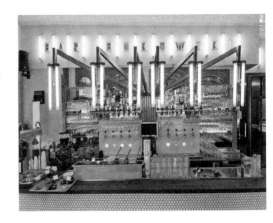

Culture · Outdoors · Night | Urban Tropical

Amsterdam Roest is a city beach located on the east side of Amsterdam. Wander into this industrial area full of old warehouses, factories and docks, and you can immediately feel the creative vibe. Next to the entrance you'll find a red double-decker bus-turned-mobile kitchen called the *Red Snack*. The menu is stacked with hearty, organic comfort food. On the waterfront behind the warehouses relax with friends at one of the tables or on a blanket in the sand. Summer-in-the-city feeling guaranteed all year long.
• Amsterdam Roest, Jacob Bontiusplaats, Oost, amsterdamroest.nl

Food | Simply Elegant

Restaurant Rijsel was one of the first champion restaurants to open its doors in up-and-coming Amsterdam East. This little beauty is located on a residential street in a building once home to the domestic science school. The interior design at Rijsel is simple but elegant—think vintage furniture, white tablecloths, a natural colour palette and an open kitchen. The concept is based on a passion for French cooking. The result: a no-nonsense menu—affordable and cooked to perfection (a three-course menu costs just under 35 euros). Since opening Rijsel has been fully booked every night, so be sure to reserve your table in advance.
• Rijsel, Marcusstraat 52B, Oost, rijsel.com

Night | Eat, Club, Sleep, Repeat

Amsterdam does an excellent job protecting its landmark buildings. Some of the most interesting food and drinks concepts are located in old constructions formerly used for something entirely different: old warehouses transform into clubs, tram sheds become food markets and factories now house the best restaurants. One of the most spectacular renovations of late is the *Volkshotel*. This design hotel was once home to one of the largest newspapers in The Netherlands, the "Volkskrant". After years of renovations, this special venue has finally opened its doors. The Volkshotel has 172 rooms, all of which are outfitted in glass, concrete and wood. There are also nine specialty rooms designed by artists and friends of the establishment—fancy sleeping in a cargo bike? One extra-special asset of this vibrant spot is the "Badplaats" area on the eighth-floor rooftop. Here, guests can enjoy hot tubs and saunas while taking in views of the city. One floor down is restaurant and club *Canvas*. This hot spot boasts a modern, affordable menu. Even better, from 11pm it turns into a club where you can dance into the early hours. Since opening, Volkshotel has proven itself to visitors and locals alike—staking a place atop the list of trendy and affordable places to stay.

• Volkshotel, Wibautstraat 150, Oost, volkshotel.nl

Bas Wiegel

The Essence of Cooking

Bas Wiegel
The chef de cuisine of Amsterdam's De Kas restaurant, Bas started his career at the bottom of the culinary food chain when he was 14, washing dishes in a small restaurant in the evenings while studying pastry making during the day. By the time he graduated, Wiegel realised he wanted to cook for a living. He trained as a chef for another six years, which involved hours of hard work and very little free time. Not that it bothered him. Wiegel says it's the pressure and adrenaline (and, of course, the ability to make his guests happy) that he loves. You can sense it immediately when you meet him—and you can taste it in his creations

Amsterdam is always on the move—and that's not just the residents zooming around on their bicycles. The city embraces a constant process of renewal and reinvention. Born to satisfy the hordes of tourists that descend on the city, there's always something new to see and new to explore in this vibrant capital. It was this diversity and energy that drew Bas Wiegel to Amsterdam, and it's Amsterdam's culinary landscape that Bas Wiegel himself has helped to shape

What is food for you?

Something very important. I personally like to eat healthily and differently. Food should make you feel good and ready for everyday life. And it's also a social thing to do with friends and family. With regards to my profession, food is my way of life; it's my job and my passion—I use food to make my guests happy and give them a special experience.

Special is a good word. You are the chef de cuisine of De Kas, which is anything but an ordinary restaurant.

Indeed, it's quite the contrary. It's very special. *De Kas* is located in a greenhouse that belonged to Amsterdam's municipal nursery in the beginning of the 20th century. Part of it has been changed into the restaurant—kitchen, dining area—while the other part still serves as a greenhouse. We grow most of our vegetables, fruits and herbs there ourselves, so everything we use is in season, harvested in the morning and served the very same day. That's why we're able to serve a surprisingly fresh menu every day.

You are in charge of creating the menus. What inspires you to make the mesmerising menus that De Kas is known for?

Together with Jarno von den Broek, who is the head chef, I make one menu every week. It is always based on the vegetables that are ripe. And when relying on nature, you never know what comes in from the land in the morning. So, it's basically nature telling us how to do the menu. We will use whatever nature provides us with. Although we also go out for dinner often and look around at what different chef colleagues are doing, that's more field research than a source of inspiration. We will always do our own thing and we don't follow other restaurants. It's a great source of inspiration to work with different products and talk with your kitchen staff. And the wine has a great say, too, as the menu and wine always need to complement each other.

So, you don't only think about what will be on the plate, but in the glass as well.

Yes, as it is important for me to have something to drink that matches with the food. When your drink is paired with the food, it will enlarge the flavour balance. We always taste the whole menu with all its appropriate wines before we serve it.

There is an exclusive "chef's table" in the kitchen. What's this all about?

I always say it's the best table in the restaurant. When you sit at the chef's table you'll be part of the kitchen. You will hear everything, see everything, feel the way the service is going, see how concentrated the chefs are. I think it's a unique experience. We always try to arrange it so that every chef in the kitchen serves one dish and explains what's special about it. We keep no secrets from our chef's table's guests—sitting there means you are part of the team.

Do you have a favorite ingredient?

Absolutely, yes. Two, in fact. Both are very simple ingredients that make vegetables taste better: zest of lemon and, of course, salt—not the white but grey salt. When you combine zest and salt with fresh vegetables your flavor will be better. Salt helps give the vegetable an extra push of flavor and the zest of lemon makes it fresh.

And where can you get fresh ingredients apart from your greenhouse at De Kas? Is there a good food market?

I always like to walk around the

Restaurant De Kas is located in an old greenhouse in Frankendael Park. The dining room is designed by Piet Boon

A social consensus: the Dutch love herring. Stubbe is a prefered supplier

Albert Cuyp Market. The fish, meat and vegetables are fresh and good. And it's just a nice place. Even when you're a local, that's a place to visit. And I'm looking forward to the *Foodhallen*—a new indoor food market that is just being built into an old holding for trams.

People expect to have very good cheese, Dutch fries and Frikandels in Amsterdam. What is your favourite traditional dish?

"Broodje haring met ui"—herring in white bread with onions. I always get one when I'm in the city.

Where exactly?

At a little kiosk called Stubbe's that's always put up by the bridge connecting the *Nieuwendijk* with the Haarlemmerstraat. It's close to the central station.

With the population of Amsterdam so diverse, that means a diverse culinary scene. For example, the city is know for its Indonesian restaurants. Which one's your favourite?

I recommend *Restaurant Blauw*. It's very authentic, good and tasty.

What are the latest restaurant and food trends in Amsterdam you're seeing?

It's leaning towards showing your guests that you're working with local produce that makes use of fair trade practices. People more and more ask for food that comes from a local farm, especially when it's meat. And everything should be as fresh as possible. The general appreciation for healthy food is literally growing. This is something I like to see and observe!

You mentioned that drinks help perfect each menu. What about drinks that go without food? Where do you get your coffee during the day and where do you go for a cocktail at night?

For coffee, I go to *Cafe Kuijper*. That's in the east. For a cocktail, I go to *Door 74*, but you definitely have to make a reservation there. Or to the *Okura Hotel*. That's also nice. Their bar is on the top of the building and offers a nice view of the skyline.

What other places would you say someone must see?

De Kas, of course. The Negen Straatjes, the *Rijksmuseum*, a tour around the canals and cycling through the north and its small villages up there.

The Dutch Touch

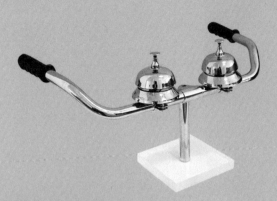

The New Sound of Cycling

This typically Dutch accessory will make you look like a Amsterdammer. The gadget is simply a hotel reception bell designed to be mounted on a bike. *Hotelfietsbel* has been designing the bells since 2011, adding new sounds to the Amsterdam experience.
• Hotelfietsbel, hotelfietsbel.nl

Then There Was Light

Vintage inspired lighting at its finest—the two Dutch brothers behind *Blom & Blom* collect, restore, and redesign industrial lamps and furnishings from forgotten factories. A passion for "authentic items with a story to tell" is the driving force behind their mission to give new life to objects from these industrial ghost towns.
• Blom & Blom, blomandblom.com

Blow Away Vase

Blue Delft Porcelain is typically from Amsterdam, but in this case, even though the pattern has stayed the same, the design of this vase breaks all the rules. Designed by *Front,* it uses wind as its inspiration, incorporating the idea of motion into its curves. This special porcelain piece proudly stands undefeated.
• Moooi, moooi.com

The Purely Genever

Once made for the Royal family and now accessible to all, this last little Amsterdam brewery brings you an excellent malt wine, or "korenwijn", the spirit that eventually evolved into gin. In this distillery the old Genever recipes haven't changed since 1900.
• A. van Wees Distilleerderij De Ooievaar, de-ooievaar.nl

Books

Dammed
• L. G. Rivera, 2011

A trip to Amsterdam leads two work companions into a whole new world of discovery: the hidden pleasures of the city and the fragility of mental sanity. "Dammed" fills the reader's imagination with exalting experiences and a subtle downward spiral into the darkness of one's own mind.

Amsterdam!
• Ed van Der Elsken, 1979

Ed van Der Elsken has perfectly captured the everyday lifestyle of post-war Amsterdam. The iconic Dutch photographer's street photography gives us a beautiful glimpse of the capital through the faces of its inhabitants over the decades.

Outsider in Amsterdam
• Janwillem Van De Wetering, 1975

A murder mystery set in the streets of Amsterdam sheds light on a newly developed religious commune. This gripping novel manages to transcend the moral dilemmas of the open drug culture of the city in the 1970s.

Movies

Amsterdamned
• Dick Maas (writer, director, music composer), 1988

Blood, thrills, explosions. This typical 1980s action film lets you explore the streets and canals of Amsterdam by way of a cliffhanging serial murder investigation. The intense speedboat chase serves up an in-depth tour of the city.

Turkish Delight
• Paul Verhoeven (director), 1973

A sex scene in the rain and Rutger Hauer riding a bicycle through the streets of Amsterdam—what could be more Dutch? Based on a novel by Jan Wolkers, this film has become a Dutch classic, portraying the era of sexual liberation in the capital.

Borgman
• Alex van Warmerdam (director, writer), 2013

A luxurious residential area just outside of Amsterdam provides the perfect juxtaposition for this absurd story. Watch the psychological games unfold in this wonderfully twisted tale.

Music

My Way
• Herman Brood, 2001

This Dutch enfant terrible's last album is arguably his best. Released posthumously, it mixes sounds from a range of rock and blues greats, from Chet Baker to Sid Vicious. In his interpretations of these classics you can hear the strain in his voice, only intensified by his drug habit at the time, which eventually led him to suicide in 2001.

The Kyteman Orchestra
• The Kyteman Orchestra, 2012

Okay, the brain behind The Orchestra, Colin Benders, is not from Amsterdam, but Utrecht. But he and the other 18 musicians, singers and choir members create an utterly unique experience, not to be missed. Lose yourself in this otherworldly blend of soul, hip-hop, pop and classical music.

Cabinet Of Curiosities
• Jacco Gardner, 2013

This young man from Hoorn, just north of Amsterdam, keeps the Hippie spirit alive. With his music he digs deep into the heritage of the sound of 1960s psychedelica.

Conservatorium

Situated next to Vondelpark and the Van Gogh Museum, the Conservatorium Hotel brings you the best of modern design wrapped up in a traditional hotel experience. Housed in the Amsterdam's former Sweelinck Conservatorium of Music, the grandeur of the building is accentuated by the design-work of Piero Lissoni. Throughout the establishment you feel surrounded by the contemporary cultural heritage of the city. However, the hotel still manages to keep a unique Dutch experience through its clean minimalist layout, subtly coupled with a variety of traditionally Dutch objects and accessories.

citizenM

The citizenM hotel is located in the quiet, southern part of the city and is renowned for its unique customer experience. The overall concept of the hotel is to mix comfort, technology and design. Each room is equipped with top-of-the-line, high-tech devices. On the ground floor, the hotel lobby is redefined: this spacious social area is full of stunning designer furniture, interesting books and free-to-use electronic devices. citizenM's guests are very likely to feel at home in the welcoming lounge area, which is possibly why the bar and restaurant stays open 24/7.

Volkshotel

Setting itself apart from the traditional hotel experience, the Volkshotel adds a touch of extravagance to your stay. The surreal decor gives the hotel a uniquely artistic feel. Located in the east side of the city just a couple minutes away from trendy de Pijp district, the Volkshotel not only attracts travellers, but also lots of locals. People come to enjoy the grand café in the early afternoon, the secret cocktail bar in the evening and the rooftop club and restaurant in the wee hours of the night. LOST IN loves the Volkshotel for its welcoming, creative atmosphere—it's become a hub for designers, music producers and artists alike, guaranteeing guests an eclectic experience.

Available from LOST iN

Issue No.1   LOST iN   English edition

BERLiN BERLiN BERLiN

Art in a WWII bunker, fashion in a hidden warehouse, nouvelle Deutsch cuisine on the canal, biking on a historic airstrip, cocktails beneath a giant rocket ... Discover the city of reinvention in 38 hours.

Issue No.2   LOST iN   English edition

Paris Paris Paris Paris

A hidden vineyard in Montmartre, an African bar along the Canal, new french cuisine on the Rive Droite, breathtaking views from a rooftop bar in Ménilmontant ... Discover the Parisian "renouveau" in 38 hours.

Issue No.3   LOST iN   English edition

Amster dam Amster dam Amster dam

Artist studios in churches, a hidden bar in a burger joint, hippie beaches in the center, a restaurant in a greenhouse, thrilling views from the old docks ... Discover an Amsterdam beyond canals and coffeeshops in 38 hours.

Issue No.4   LOST iN   English edition

LON DON LON DON

A Michelin starred pub, a super-secret bar, a book club with a massive sound system, a quiet green hill to behold the city's skyline and a nighttime restaurant above the clouds... Discover an evolving London in 38 hours.

Issue No.5   LOST iN   English edition

Vienna Vienna Vienna

A secret café with an impressive vinyl collection, a disco ball pizza oven, a cemetery for the nameless, a restaurant in an old Apotheke and Europe's finest tap water... Discover Vienna from Schubert to Falco in 38 hours.

Issue No.6   LOST iN   English edition

Milan Milan Milan

A flamingo garden, slow food markets, a secret bar, traditional trattorias, hidden masterpieces of Italian design... Discover the ever changing city of Milan in 38 hours.

Issue No.7   LOST iN   English edition

BARCE LONA BARCE LONA

Tapas with a modern twist, utopian housing projects, thrilling views from a diving board, art spaces in abandoned factories, brand beaches in the outskirts... Discover the Barcelona beyond the Ramblas in 38 hours.

Issue No.8   LOST iN   English edition

NYC NYC NYC

Tropical vibes in Queens, Michelin starred viking cuisine, ice-cold Martinis in Kennedy's haunt, Brooklyn handcrafted jeans, beach life with The Boss, dolce vita in the Bronx... Discover the sparkling city of New York in 38 hours.

Issue No.9   LOST iN   English edition

Frank furt Frank furt

Fine dining in a kiosk, a graffitied cave under the autobahn, a modernist housing project, a secret speak easy bar, an unbuilt tower by Mies van der Rohe... Discover the creative force behind Frankfurt in 38 hours.

Next Issue: Los Angeles

WWW.LOSTIN.COM

Index

© Culture
Ⓕ Food
Ⓝ Night
Ⓞ Outdoors
Ⓢ Shop

De Pijp

Club 8
Admiraal de
Ruijterweg 56B
+31.(0)20.685 17 03
club-8.nl
→ p. 16 Ⓝ

**NASA: New Art Space
Amsterdam.**
Arie Biemondstraat
111
+31.(0)20.427 59 51
NASAhq.net
→ p. 15 Ⓒ

Pacific Parc
Polonceaukade 23
+31.(0)20.488 77 78
pacificparc.nl
→ p. 48 Ⓝ

Westerliefde
Klonne plein 4-6
+31.(0)20.684 84 96
westerliefde.nl
→ p. 48 Ⓕ Ⓝ

Pont 13
Haparandadam 50
+31.(0)20.770 27 22
pont13.nl
→ p. 15 Ⓕ

Mossel & Gin
Gosschalklaan 12
+31.(0)20.486 58 69
mosselengin.nl
→ p. 47 Ⓕ Ⓝ

Centrum

Baskets
Elandsgracht 57
+31.(0)20.428 40 71
basketsamsterdam.
com
→ p. 23 Ⓢ

Brasserie Schiller
Rembrandtplein 26
+31.(0)20.554 07 23
brasserieschiller.nl
→ p. 32 Ⓕ

Stubbe Haring Kiosk
Singel Haarlingersluis
→ p. 57 Ⓕ

Concrete Matter
Haarlemmerdijk 127
+31.(0)20.261 09 33
concrete-matter.com
→ p. 23 Ⓢ Ⓕ

Oude Kerk
Oudekerksplein 23
+31.(0)20.625 82 84
oudekerk.nl
→ p. 31 Ⓒ

A. Boeken
Nieuwe
Hoogstraat 31
+31.(0)20.626 72 05
aboeken.nl
→ p. 48 Ⓢ

De Appel Arts Center
Prins
Hendrikkade 142
+31.(0)20.625 56 51
deappel.nl
→ p. 15 Ⓒ

De Engelse Reet
Begijnensteeg 4
+31.(0)20.623 17 77
→ p. 16 Ⓝ

De Koffieschenkerij
Oudekerksplein 27
+31.(0)64.129 81 14
→ p. 48

Door 74
Reguliersdwarsstraat
741
31(0) 63. 404 51 22
door-74.com
→ p. 57 Ⓝ

FOAM
izersgracht 609
+31.(0)20.551 65 00
foam.org
→ p. 10 Ⓒ

G's Brunch Boat
Goudsbloemstraat 91
reallyniceplace.com
→ p. 11 Ⓕ

Hortus Botanicus
Plantage
Middenlaan 2a
+31.(0)20.625 90 21
dehortus.nl
→ p. 31 Ⓞ

Droog
Staalstraat 7-A
31(0) 20. 523 50 59
droog.com
→ p. 9, p.47 Ⓢ

Ibericus
Haarlemmerstraat 93
+31.(0)20.223 65 73
→ p. 11 Ⓢ

Leonore
Utrechtsestraat 53
+31.(0)20.624 56 55
leonoresieraden.nl
→ p. 47 Ⓢ

Nacional
Gartmanplantsoen 11
+31.(0)20.205 09 08
nacional.nl
→ p. 24 Ⓕ Ⓢ

**Noordermarkt feat.
Boerenmarkt**
Buikslotermeerplein
boerenmarktnoord.nl
→ p. 10 Ⓢ

**Ons' Lieve Heer
op Solder**
Oudezijds
Voorburgwal 40
+31.(0)20.624 66 04
opsolder.nl
→ p. 15 Ⓒ

Puccini Bomboni
Singel 184
+31.(0)20.427 83 41
puccinibomboni.com
→ p. 16 Ⓕ Ⓢ

Quartier Putain
Oudekerksplein 4
quartierputain.nl
→ p. 47 Ⓕ Ⓝ

Restored
Haarlemmerdijk 39
+31.(0)20.337 64 73
restored.nl
→ p. 11 Ⓢ

Stach
Van Woustraat 154
+31.(0)20.754 26 72
stach-food.nl
→ p. 11 Ⓢ

Six & Sons
Haarlemmerdijk 31
+31.(0)20.233 00 92
sixandsons.com
→ p. 11, p.23 Ⓢ

Sukha
Haarlemmerstraat
110
+31.(0)20.664 54 78
sukha-amsterdam.nl
→ p. 11 Ⓢ

Tales & spirits
Lijnbaanssteeg 5
+31(0) 65. 535 64 67
talesandspirits.com
→ p. 48 Ⓝ

Tenue de Nimes
Haarlemmerstraat
92–94
+31.(0)20.320 40 12
tenuedenimes.com
→ p. 11 Ⓢ

Tommy Page Vintage
Prinsenstraat 7
+31.(0)20.330 79 41
tommypage.nl
→ p. 23 Ⓢ

Tweede Kamer
Heisteeg 6

Unlimited Delicious
Haarlemmerstraat
122
+31.(0)20.622 48 29
unlimiteddelicious.nl
→ p. 16 Ⓕ

W139
Warmoesstraat 139
+31.(0)20.622 94 34
w139.nl
→ p. 15 Ⓒ

Oost

Bar Bukowski
Oosterpark 10
+31.(0)20.370 16 85
barbukowski.nl
→ p. 52 Ⓝ Ⓕ

Cafe Kuijper
Linnaeusstraat 79
+31.(0)20.665 19 26
cafekuijper.nl
→ p. 57 Ⓕ

De Kas
Kamerlingh
Onneslaan 3
+31.(0)20.462 45 62
restaurantdekas.nl
→ p. 55 Ⓕ

Henry's Bar
Oosterpark 11
+31.(0)20.370 16 85
henrysbar.nl
→ p. 52 Ⓝ Ⓕ

Hoftuin
Nieuwe
Herengracht 18
+31.(0)20.370 27 23
hoftuin.com
→ p. 32 Ⓕ

Rijsel
Marcusstraat 52B
+31.(0)20.463 21 42
rijsel.com
→ p. 52 Ⓕ

Amsterdam Roest
Jacob Bontiusplaats 1
+31.(0)20.308 02 83
amsterdamroest.nl
→ p. 52 Ⓝ

ON THE ROAD

The App for the Discerning Traveller

Explore insider recommendations and create your personal itinerary with handpicked locations tailored to your desires. Our selection of experiences ranges from independent boutiques, galleries and neighborhood bars to brand new restaurants. Experience a new city from within.

LOST iN